Let Me

TRICIA SYBERSMA

Designed by Rachel Rossano

TRICIA SYBERSMA

COPYRIGHT © 2022 BY TRICIA SYBERSMA
DESIGN AND LAYOUT BY RACHEL ROSSANO
ALL IMAGERY FROM SHUTTERSTOCK.COM

ALL RIGHTS RESERVED. NO PART OF THIS BOOK MAY BE REPRODUCED, STORED IN A RETRIEVAL SYSTEM, OR TRANSMITTED IN ANY FORM OR BY ANY MEANS—ELECTRONIC, MECHANICAL, PHOTOCOPY, RECORDING, OR OTHERWISE—WITHOUT THE PRIOR PERMISSION OF THE PUBLISHER OR AUTHOR.

THE ONLY EXCEPTION IS BY A REVIEWER, WHO MAY QUOTE SHORT EXCERPTS IN A REVIEW.

CONTACT THE AUTHOR AT: TRICIA@TRICIASYBERSMA.COM

PRINT ISBN: 978-1-948074-69-8

EBOOK ISBN: 978-1-948074-67-4

FIRST EDITION

"A love letter from the Earth"

Dedicated to all who call "Earth" home

Let me
be the ground beneath your feet,

Let me comfort you on my soft grasses.

Let me relax you on my white sands,

Let me refresh you in my calm, clear waters.

Let me

cool you under the shade of my trees,
Let me fill your ears with the songs of my birds.

Let me tickle your nose with

the essences of my flowers,

Let me light up your eyes with

the colours of my rainbows.

Let me

satisfy your touch,

with the softness of my flower petals,

the prickliness of my thorns,

the smoothness of my sun-warmed rocks.

Let me
cleanse you with my rain,

Let me renew you with my storms,

Let me warm you with my fire.

Let me
feed your body from my soil,

Let me quench your thirst from my streams.

Let me be your bed while gazing at the stars in the sky,

Let me hold you as you soak up my sun.

Let me

give you shelter with my mud, wood, and stone,

Let me give you tools from my metals,

Let me clothe you with my bamboo, hemp, and cotton.

Let me give you companionship with my animals,

Let me give you beauty and energy with my crystals,

Let me give you medicine with my herbs.

Let me show you fragility and grace with my butterflies,
Let me show you power and might with my stormy seas.

Let me

give you the day to work,

Let me give you the night to rest.

Let me be your compass,

Let me share with you the secrets of the universe.

Let me

be your teacher in all things big and small,

Let me hug you with my strong tree trunks

and branches.

Let me give you healing with a simple touch,

Let me give you...love.

~ The Earth

About the author

TRICIA SYBERSMA

Tricia was born in Toronto and grew up in Blue Mountain, Ontario. In 1993, Tricia and her family moved to the Cayman Islands, where she continues to reside.

Whether surrounded by sandy beaches, meadows, apples trees or snow, Tricia looks for the magic that is just beyond our awareness, then brings it to life with her poems and stories.

Tricia is a HeartMath® Certified Trainer
Visit TriciaSybersma.com

ABOUT THE DESIGNER – RACHEL ROSSANO

Rachel grew up in the beautiful Niagara Region in Ontario, Canada. She has been designing and art directing for 16 years and can be reached at RachelRossano.ca